Narrative of
My Escape
from Slavery

Narrative of My Escape from Slavery

Moses Roper

DOVER PUBLICATIONS, INC.
Mineola, New York

Bibliographical Note

Moses Roper's book, under the title *A Narrative of the Escape of Moses Roper, from American Slavery,* was first published in London by Darton, Harvey and Darton in 1837. Between then and 1856, it went through no fewer than ten editions. The first American publication was by Merrihew & Gunn, Philadelphia, in 1838.

This Dover edition, first published in 2003, is an unabridged republication of Darton, Harvey and Darton's second edition, published in 1838. The text is taken from the facsimile edition published by Negro Universities Press, New York, in 1970.

Library of Congress Cataloging-in-Publication Data

Roper, Moses.
    [Narrative of the adventures and escape of Moses Roper from American slavery]
    Narrative of my escape from slavery / Moses Roper.
       p. cm.
    Originally published: A narrative of the adventures and escape of Moses Roper from American slavery. 2nd ed. London : Darton, Harvey, and Darton, 1838.
    ISBN-13: 978-0-486-42718-8 (pbk.)
    ISBN-10: 0-486-42718-8 (pbk.)

    1. Roper, Moses. 2. Slaves—United States—Biography. 3. Fugitive slaves—United States—Biography. 4. African Americans—Biography. 5. Racially mixed people—United States—Biography. 6. Slavery—South Carolina—History. 7. Slaves—South Carolina—Social conditions—Case studies. 8. Liberty Hill Region (S.C.)—Biography. I. Title.

E444 .R785 2003
305.5'67'092—dc21
[B]   2002031544

Manufactured in the United States by LSC Communications
42718809   2018
www.doverpublications.com

Advertisement
to the
SECOND EDITION

The encouragement which the Author of the following "Narrative" has met with, in the sale of the First Edition, for which he desires to express his sincere gratitude, and the urgent calls which are still made from the provincial towns and in the metropolis, for more copies, have induced him to put forth this Second Edition, by the sale of which, he fully anticipates the realization of his object: namely, to create a fund which may enable him to qualify himself to instruct the heathen, and to acquaint the English reader with some of the evils of the slavery system in America.

The Author cannot omit this opportunity of stating, with a deep feeling of gratitude, that the publication of the first edition of this work has induced a gentleman of Manchester, previously a stranger to him, most generously to send out the pecuniary means for releasing one of his sisters from slavery, who is mentioned in p. 13.

London,
1st January, 1838.

Preface

The following narrative was to have appeared under the auspices of the Rev. Dr. Morison, of Chelsea, whose generous exertions on behalf of Moses Roper have entitled him to the admiration and gratitude of every philanthropist. But the illness of the doctor having prevented him from reading the manuscript, I have been requested to supply his lack of service. To this request I assent reluctantly, as the narrative would have derived a fuller sanction and wider currency, had circumstances permitted the original purpose to be carried out. Moses Roper was introduced to Dr. Morison, by an eminent American abolitionist, in a letter, dated November 9th, 1835, in which honourable testimony is borne to his general character, and the soundness of his religious profession. "He has spent about ten days in my house," says Dr. Morison's correspondent, "I have watched him attentively, and have no doubt, that he is an excellent young man, that he possesses uncommon intelligence, sincere piety, and a strong desire to preach the Gospel. He can tell you his own story better than any one else, and I believe, that if he should receive an education, he would be able to counteract the false and wicked misrepresentations of American slavery, which are made in your country by our Priests and Levites who visit you."

Dr. Morison, as might have been anticipated from his well-known character, heartily responded to the appeal of his American correspondent. He sent his letter to the *Patriot* Newspaper, remarking in his own communication to the Editor, "I have seen Moses Roper, the fugitive slave. He comes to this country, as you will perceive, well authenticated as to character and religious standing; and my anxiety is, that the means may forthwith be supplied by some of your generous readers, for placing him in some appropriate seminary for the improvement of his mind, that he may be trained for future usefulness in the church. His thirst for knowledge is great; and he may yet become a most important agent in liberating his country from the curse of slavery."

Moses Roper brought with him to this country several other testimonies, from persons residing in different parts of the States; but it is unnecessary to extend this Preface by quoting them. They all speak the same language, and bear unequivocal witness to his sobriety, intelligence, and honesty.

He is now in the land of freedom, and is earnestly desirous of availing himself of the advantages of his position. His great ambition is to be qualified for usefulness amongst his own people; and the progress he has already made, justifies the belief, that, if the means of education can be secured for a short time longer, he will be eminently qualified to instruct the children of Africa in the truths of the gospel of Christ. He has drawn up the following narrative, partly with the hope of being assisted in this legitimate object, and partly to engage the sympathies of our countrymen on behalf of his oppressed brethren. I trust that he will not be disappointed in either of these expectations, but that all the friends of humanity and religion among us, will cheerfully render him their aid, by promoting the circulation of his volume. Should this be done to the extent that is quite possible, the difficulties now lying in his way will be removed.

Of the narrative itself it is not necessary that I should say much. It is his own production, and carries with it internal evidence of truth. Some of its statements will probably startle those readers who are unacquainted with the details of the slave system; but no such feeling will be produced in any who are conversant with the practice of slavery, whether in America or our own colonies. There is no vice too loathsome—no passion too cruel or remorseless, to be engendered by this horrid system. It brutalizes all who administer it, and seeks to efface the likeness of God, stamped on the brow of its victims. It makes the former class demons, and reduces the latter to the level of brutes.

I could easily adduce from the records of our own slave system, as well as from those of America, several instances of equal
atrocity to any which Moses Roper has recorded. But this is
unnecessary, and I shall, therefore, merely add, the unqualified
expression of my own confidence in the truth of this narrative,
and my strong recommendation of it to the patronage of the
British Public.

THOMAS PRICE.

HACKNEY, July 22nd, 1837.

Introduction

The determination of laying this little narrative before the public, did not arise from any desire to make myself conspicuous, but with the view of exposing the cruel system of slavery as will here be laid before my readers; from the urgent calls of nearly all the friends to whom I had related any part of the story, and also from the recommendation of anti-slavery meetings, which I have attended, through the suggestion of many warm friends of the cause of the oppressed.

The general narrative, I am aware, may seem to many of my readers, and especially to those, who have not been before put in possession of the actual features of this accursed system, somewhat at variance with the dictates of humanity. But the facts related here, do not come before the reader, unsubstantiated by collateral evidence, nor highly coloured to the disadvantage of cruel task-masters.

My readers may be put in possession of facts respecting this system which equal in cruelty my own narrative, on an authority which may be investigated with the greatest satisfaction. Besides which, this little book will not be confined to a small circle of my own friends in London, or even in England. The slave-holder, the colonizationist, and even Mr. Gooch himself, will be able to obtain this document, and be at liberty to draw from it whatever they are honestly able, in order to set me down as the tool of a party. Yea, even friend Brechenridge, a gentleman known at Glasgow, will be able to possess this, and to draw from it all the forcible arguments on his own side, which in his wisdom, honesty, and candour he may be able to adduce.

The earnest wish to lay this narrative before my friends as an impartial statement of facts, has led me to develope some part of my conduct, which I now deeply deplore. The ignorance in which the poor slaves are kept by their masters, preclude almost the possibility of their being alive to any moral duties.

With these remarks, I leave the statement before the public. May this little volume be the instrument of opening the eyes of the ignorant to this system—of convincing the wicked, cruel, and hardened slave-holder—and of befriending generally the cause of oppressed humanity.

MOSES ROPER.

London,
June 28, 1837.

Narrative of
My Escape
from Slavery

"By our sufferings, since ye brought us
To the man-degrading mart;
All sustained by patience, taught us
Only by a broken heart."

Escape, &c.

I was born in North Carolina, in Caswell County, I am not able to tell in what year or month. What I shall now relate, is, what was told me by my mother and grandmother. A few months before I was born, my father married my mother's young mistress. As soon as my father's wife heard of my birth, she sent one of my mother's sisters to see whether I was white or black, and when my aunt had seen me, she returned back as soon as she could, and told her mistress that I was white, and resembled Mr. Roper very much. Mr. R.'s wife being not pleased with this report, she got a large club stick and knife, and hastened to the place in which my mother was confined. She went into my mother's room with full intention to murder me with her knife and club, but as she was going to stick the knife into me, my grandmother happening to come in, caught the knife, and saved my life. But as well as I can recollect from what my mother told me, my father sold her and myself soon after her confinement. I cannot recollect, any thing that is worth notice, till I was six or seven years old. My mother being half white, and my father a white man, I was at that time very white. Soon after I was six or seven years of age, my mother's old master died, that is, my father's wife's father. All his slaves had to be divided among the children.* I have mentioned before of my father disposing of me, I am not sure whether he exchanged me and my mother for

---

*Slaves are usually a part of the marriage portion, but lent rather than given, to be returned to the estate at his decease of the father, in order that they may be divided equally among his children.

another slave or not, but think it very likely he did exchange me with one of his wife's brothers or sisters, because I remember when my mother's old master died, I was living with my father's wife's brother-in-law, whose name was Mr. Durham. My mother was drawn with the other slaves.

The way they divide their slaves is this: they write the names of different slaves on a small piece of paper, and put it into a box and let them all draw. I think that Mr. Durham drew my mother, and Mr. Fowler drew me, so we were separated a considerable distance, I cannot say how far. My resembling my father so very much, and being whiter than the other slaves, caused me to be soon sold to what they call a negro trader, who took me to the Southern States of America, several hundred miles from my mother. As well as I can recollect, I was then about six years old. The trader, Mr. Mitchell, after travelling several hundred miles, and selling a good many of his slaves, found he could not sell me very well, (as I was so much whiter than the other slaves were) for he had been trying several months—left me with a Mr. Sneed, who kept a large boarding-house, who took me to wait at table, and sell me if he could. I think I stayed with Mr. Sneed about a year, but he could not sell me. When Mr. Mitchell had sold his slaves, he went to the north, and brought up another drove, and returned to the south with them, and sent his son-in-law into Washington, in Georgia, after me, so he came and took me from Mr. Sneed, and met his father-in-law with me, in a town called Lancaster, with his drove of slaves. We stayed in Lancaster a week, because it was court week, and there were a great many people there, and it was a good opportunity for selling the slaves, and there he was enabled to sell me to a gentleman, Dr. Jones, who was both a Doctor and a Cotton Planter. He took me into his shop to beat up and to mix medicines, which was not a very hard employment, but I did not keep it long, as the Doctor soon sent me to his Cotton plantation, that I might be burnt darker by the sun. He sent for me to be with a tailor to learn the trade, but all the journeymen being white men, Mr. Bryant, the tailor, did not let me work in the shop; I cannot say whether it was the prejudice of his journeymen, in not wanting me to sit in the shop with them, or whether Mr.

Bryant wanted to keep me about the house to do the domestic work, instead of teaching me the trade. After several months, my master came to know how I got on with the trade: I am not able to tell Mr. Bryant's answer, but it was either that I could not learn, or that his journeymen were not willing that I should sit in the shop with them. I was only once in the shop all the time I was there, and then only for an hour or two, before his wife called me out to do some other work. So my master took me home, and as he was going to send a load of cotton to Camden, about forty miles distance, he sent me with the bales of cotton to be sold with it, where I was soon sold to a gentleman, named Allen, but Mr. Allen soon exchanged me for a female slave, to please his wife. The traders who bought me, were named Cooper and Linsey, who took me for sale, but could not sell me, people objecting to my being rather white. They then took me to the city of Fayetteville, North Carolina, where he swopt me for a boy, that was blacker than me, to Mr. Smith, who lived several miles off.

I was with Mr. Smith nearly a year. I arrived at the first knowledge of my age when I lived with him. I was then between twelve and thirteen years old, it was when President Jackson was elected the first time, and he has been president eight years, so I must be nearly twenty-one years of age. At this time, I was quite a small boy, and was sold to Mr. Hodge, a negro trader. Here I began to enter into hardships. After travelling several hundred miles, Mr. Hodge, sold me to Mr. Gooch the cotton-planter, Cashaw County, South Carolina, he purchased me at a town called Liberty Hill, about three miles from his home. As soon as he got home, he immediately put me on his cotton plantation to work, and put me under overseers, gave me allowance of meat and bread with the other slaves, which was not half enough for me to live upon, and very laborious work; here my heart was almost broke with grief at leaving my fellow-slaves. Mr. Gooch did not mind my grief, for he flogged me nearly every day, and very severely. Mr. Gooch bought me for his son-in-law, Mr. Hammans, about five miles from his residence. This man had but two slaves besides myself, he treated me very kindly for a week or two, but in summer when cotton was ready to hoe, he gave me task work, connected with this department, which I could not get done, not having worked on cotton farms before. When I failed in my task he commenced flogging me, and set me to work without any shirt, in the cotton field, in a very hot sun, in the month of July. In August, Mr. Condell, his overseer, gave me a task at pulling fodder; having finished my task before night, I left the field, the rain came on which soaked the fodder, on discovering this, he threatened to flog me for not getting in the fodder before the rain came. This was the first time I attempted to run away, knowing that I should get a flogging. I was then between thirteen and fourteen years of age, I ran away to the woods half naked, I was caught by a slave-holder, who put me in Lancaster Gaol. When they put slaves in gaol, they advertise for their masters to own them; but if the master does not claim his slave in six months, from the time of imprisonment, the slave is sold for gaol fees. When the slave runs away, the master always adopts a more rigorous system of flogging, this was the case in the present instance. After this, having determined from my youth to gain my freedom, I made several attempts, was caught, and got a severe flogging of 100 lashes, each time. Mr. Hammans was a very severe and cruel master, and his wife still worse, she used to tie me up and flog me while naked.

After Mr. Hammans saw that I was determined to die in the woods, and not live with him, he tried to obtain a piece of land from his father-in-law, Mr. Gooch; not having the means of purchasing it, he exchanged me for the land.

As soon as Mr. Gooch had possession of me again, knowing that I was averse to going back to him, he chained me by the neck to his chaise. In this manner he took me to his home at Mac Daniel's Ferry, in the County of Chester, a distance of fifteen miles. After which, he put me in a swamp, to cut trees, the heaviest work, which men of twenty-five or thirty years of age have to do, I being but sixteen. Here I was on very short allowance of food, and having heavy work, was too weak to fulfil my tasks. For this I got many severe floggings; and after I had got my irons off, I made another attempt at running away. He took my irons off in the full anticipation that I could never get across the Catarba River, even when at liberty. On this, I procured a small Indian canoe, which was tied to a tree, and ultimately got across the river in it. I then wandered through the wilderness for several days without any food, and but a drop of water to allay my thirst, till I became so starved, that I was obliged to go to a house to beg for something to eat, when I was captured, and again imprisoned.

Mr. Gooch having heard of me through an advertisement, sent his son after me; he tied me up and took me back to his father. Mr. Gooch then obtained the assistance of another slaveholder, and tied me up in his blacksmith's shop, and gave me fifty lashes with a cow hide. He then put a log-chain, weighing twenty-five pounds, round my neck, and sent me into a field, into which he followed me with the cow hide, intending to set his slaves to flog me again. Knowing this, and dreading to suffer again in this way, I gave him the slip, and got out of his sight, he having stopped to speak with the other slave-holder.

I got to a canal on the Catarba River, on the banks of which, and near to a lock, I procured a stone and a piece of iron, with which I forced the ring off my chain, and got it off, and then crossed the river, and walked about twenty miles, when I fell in with a slave-holder, named Ballad, who had married the sister of Mr. Hammans. I knew that he was not so cruel as Mr. Gooch, and, therefore, begged of him to buy me. Mr. Ballad, who was one of the best planters in the neighbourhood, said, that he was not able to buy me, and stated, that he was obliged to take me back to my master, on account of the heavy fine attaching to a man harbouring a slave. Mr. Ballad proceeded to take me back; as we came in sight of Mr. Gooch's, all the treatment that I had met with there, came forcibly upon my mind, the powerful influence of which is beyond description. On my knees, with tears in my eyes, with terror in my countenance, and fervency in all my features, I implored Mr. Ballad to buy me, but he again refused, and I was taken back to my dreaded and cruel master. Having reached Mr. Gooch's, he proceeded to punish me. This he did by first tying my wrists together and placing them over the knees, he then put a stick through, under my knees and over my arms, and having thus secured my arms, he proceeded to flog me, and gave me 500 lashes on my bare back. This may appear incredible, but the marks which they left, at present remain on my body, a standing testimony to the truth of this statement of his severity. He then chained me down in a log-pen with a 40 lbs. chain, and made me lie on the damp earth all night. In the morning, after his breakfast, he came to me, and without giving me any breakfast, tied me to a large heavy harrow, which is usually drawn by a horse, and made me drag it to the cotton field for the horse to use in the field. Thus, the reader will see, that it was of no possible use to my master, to make me drag it to the field and not through it; his cruelty went so far, as actually to make me the slave of his horse, and thus to degrade me. He then flogged me again, and set me to work in the corn field the whole of that day, and at night, chained me down in the log-pen as before. The next morning, he took me to the cotton field, and gave me a third flogging, and set me to hoe cotton. At this time, I was dreadfully sore and weak with the repeated floggings and harsh treatment I had endured. He put me under a black man, with orders, that if I did not keep my row up in hoeing with this man, he was to flog me. The reader must recollect here, that not being used to this kind of work, having been a domestic slave, it was quite impossible for me to keep up with him, and, therefore, I was repeatedly flogged during the day.

Mr. Gooch had a female slave about eighteen years old, who also had been a domestic slave, and through not being able to fulfil her task, had run away; which slave, he was at this time punishing for that offence. On the third day, he chained me to this female slave, with a large chain of 40 lbs.* weight round the neck. It was most harrowing to my feelings, thus to be chained to a young female slave, for whom I would rather have suffered 100 lashes, than she should have been thus treated; he kept me chained to her during the week, and repeatedly flogged us both, while thus chained together, and forced us to keep up with the

---

*This was a chain that they used to draw logs with from the woods, when they clear their land.

other slaves, although retarded by the heavy weight of the log-chain.

Here again, words are insufficient to describe the misery which possessed both body and mind, whilst under this treatment, and which was most dreadfully increased, by the sympathy which I felt for my poor degraded fellow-sufferer. On the Friday morning, I entreated my master to set me free from my chains, and promised him, to do the task which was given me, and more, if possible, if he would desist from flogging me. This he refused to do, until Saturday night, when he did set me free. This must rather be ascribed to his own interest in preserving me from death, as it was very evident, I could no longer have survived under such treatment.

After this, though still determined in my own mind to escape, I stayed with him several months, during which, he frequently flogged me but not so severely, as before related. During this time, I had opportunity for recovering my health, and using means to heal my wounds. My master's cruelty was not confined to me, it was his general conduct to all his slaves. I might relate many instances to substantiate this, but will confine myself to one or two. Mr. Gooch, it is proper to observe, was a member of a Baptist church, called Black Jack Meeting House, in Cashaw County, which church I attended for several years, but was never inside. This is accounted for, by the fact, that the coloured population are not permitted to mix with the white population. In the Roman Catholic church no distinction is made. Mr. Gooch had a slave named Phil, who was a member of a Methodist church; this man, was between seventy and eighty years of age; he was so feeble that he could not accomplish his tasks, for which, his master used to chain him round the neck, and run him down a steep hill; this treatment, he never relinquished to the time of his death. Another case, was that of a slave named Peter, who, for not doing his task, he flogged nearly to death, and afterwards pulled out his pistol to shoot him, but his (Mr. Gooch's) daughter snatched the pistol from his hand. Another mode of punishment which this man adopted was, that of using iron horns, with bells, attached to the back of the slave's neck. The following, is the instrument of torture:

A WOMAN WITH IRON HORNS AND BELLS ON,
TO KEEP HER FROM RUNNING AWAY.

This instrument he used to prevent the negroes running away, being a very ponderous machine, several feet in height, and the cross pieces being two feet four, and six feet in length. This custom is generally adopted among the slave-holders in South Carolina, and some other slave states. One morning, about an hour before day-break, I was going on an errand for my master, having proceeded about a quarter of a mile, I came up to a man, named King (Mr. Sumlin's overseer), who had caught a young girl that had run away with the above machine on her. She had proceeded four miles from her station, with the intention of getting into the hands of a more humane master. She came up with this overseer nearly dead, and could get no farther, he immediately secured her, and took her back to her master, a Mr. Johnston.

Having been in the habit of going over many slave states with my master, I had good opportunities of witnessing the harsh treatment which was adopted by masters, towards their slaves. As I have never read nor heard of any thing connected with slavery so cruel as what I have myself witnessed, it will be well to mention a case or two.

A large farmer, Colonel M'Quiller, in Cashaw County, South Carolina, was in the habit of driving nails into a hogshead, so as to leave the point of the nail, just protruding in the inside of the cask, into this he used to put his slaves for punishment, and roll them down a very long and steep hill. I have heard from several slaves (though I had no means of ascertaining the truth of the statement), that in this way, he killed six or seven of his slaves. This plan was first adopted by a Mr. Perry, who lived on the Catarba River, and has since been adopted by several planters. Another was, that of a young lad, who had been hired by Mr. Bell, a member of a Methodist church, to hoe three quarters of an acre of cotton per day. Having been brought up as a domestic slave, he was not able to accomplish the task assigned to him. On the Saturday night, he left three or four rows to do on the Sunday; on the same night, it rained very hard, by which the master could tell that he had done some of the rows on Sunday. On Monday, his master took and tied him up to a tree in the field, and kept him there the whole of that day, and flogged him at intervals. At night, when he was taken down, he was so weak that he could not get home, having a mile to go. Two white men, who were employed by Mr. Bell, put him on a horse, took him home, and threw him down on the kitchen floor, while they proceeded to their supper. In a little time, they heard some deep groans proceeding from the kitchen, they went to see him die; he had groaned his last. Thus, Mr. Bell flogged this poor boy, even to death; for what? for breaking the Sabbath, when he (his master) had set him a task, on Saturday, which it was not possible for him to do, and which, if he did not do, no mercy would be extended towards him. So much for the regard of this Methodist, for the observance of the Sabbath.* The general custom in this respect is, that if a man kills his own slave, no notice is taken of it by the civil functionaries; but if a man kills a slave, belonging to another master, he is compelled to pay the worth of the slave. In this case, a jury met, returned a verdict of "Wilful Murder" against this man, and ordered him to pay the value. Mr. Bell was unable to do this, but a Mr. Cunningham paid the debt, and took this Mr. Bell, with this recommendation for cruelty, to be his overseer.

It will be observed, that most of the cases here cited, are those in respect to males. Many instances, however, in respect

*I am happy to find that the Methodists are quite a different people in England, and I hope that they will do all that they can to enlighten their slave-holding brethren in America.

to females, might be mentioned, but are too disgusting to appear in this narrative. The cases here brought forward are not rare, but the continued feature of slavery. But I must now follow up the narrative, as regards myself, in particular. I stayed with this master for several months, during which time, we went on very well in general. In August, 1831, (this was my first acquaintance with any date;) I happened to hear a man mention this date, and, as it excited my curiosity, I asked what it meant, they told me, it was the number of the year, from the birth of Christ. On this date, August, 1831, some cows broke into a crib where the corn is kept, and ate a great deal. For this, his slaves were tied up, and received several floggings; but myself and another man, hearing the groans of those who were being flogged, stayed back in the field, and would not come up. Upon this, I thought to escape punishment. On the Monday morning, however, I heard my master flogging the other man who was in the field, he could not see me, it being a field of Indian corn, which grows to a great height. Being afraid that he would catch me, and dreading a flogging more than many others, I determined to run for it; and, after travelling forty miles, I arrived at the estate of Mr. Crawford, in North Carolina, Mecklinburgh County. Having formerly heard people talk about the Free States, I determined upon going thither, and, if possible, in my way, to find out my poor mother, who was in slavery, several hundred miles from Chester; but the hope of doing the latter, was very faint, and, even if I did, it was not likely that she would know me, having been separated from her, when between five and six years old.

The first night, I slept in a barn, upon Mr. Crawford's estate, and, having overslept myself, was awoke by Mr. Crawford's overseer, upon which, I was dreadfully frightened; he asked me, what I was doing there? I made no reply to him then, and he making sure that he had secured a run-a-way slave, did not press me for an answer. On my way to his house, however, I made up the following story, which I told him in the presence of his wife:—I said, that I had been bound to a very cruel master when I was a little boy, and that having been treated very badly, I wanted to get home to see my mother. This statement, may appear to some to be untrue, but as I understood the word *bound,* I considered it to apply to my case, having been sold to him, and thereby bound to serve him; though still I did rather hope that he would understand it, that I was bound, when a boy, till twenty-one years of age. Though I was white at that time, he would not believe my story, on account of my hair being curly and wooly, which led him to conclude, I was possessed of enslaved blood. The overseer's wife, however, who seemed much interested in me, said, she did not think I was of African origin, and that she had seen white men still darker than me, her persuasion prevailed; and, after the overseer had given me as much butter-milk as I could drink, and something to eat, which was very acceptable, having had nothing for two days, I set off for Charlotte, in North Carolina, the largest town in the county. I went on very quickly the whole of that day, fearful of being pursued. The trees were very thick on each side of the road, and only a few houses, at the distance of two or three miles apart: as I proceeded, I turned round in all directions, to see if I was pursued, and if I caught a glimpse of any one coming along the road, I immediately rushed into the thickest part of the wood, to elude the grasp, of what I was afraid, might be my master. I went on in this way the whole day, at night, I came up with two waggons, they had been to market, the regular road waggons do not generally put up at inns, but encamp in the roads and fields. When I came to them, I told them the same story I had told Mr. Crawford's overseer, with the assurance, that the statement would meet the same success. After they had heard me, they gave me something to eat, and also a lodging in the camp with them.

I then went on with them about five miles, and they agreed to take me with them as far as they went, if I would assist them. This I promised to do. In the morning, however, I was much frightened by one of the men putting several questions to me— we were then about three miles from Charlotte. When within a mile of that town, we stopped at a brook, to water the horses; while stopping there, I saw the men whispering, and fancying I overheard them say, they would put me in Charlotte gaol, when they got there, I made my escape into the woods, pretending to be looking after something, till I got out of their sight. I then ran on as fast as I could, but did not go through the town of Charlotte as had been my intention; being a large town, I was fearful it might prove fatal to my escape. Here, I was at a loss how to get on, as houses were not very distant from each other, for nearly 200 miles.

While thinking what I should do, I observed some waggons before me, which I determined to keep behind, and never go nearer to them than a quarter of a mile—in this way I travelled, till I got to Salisbury. If I happened to meet any person on the road, I was afraid they would take me up, I asked them, how far the waggons had got on before me? to make them suppose, I belonged to the waggons. At night, I slept on the ground in the woods, some little distance from the waggons, but not near enough, to be seen by the men belonging to them. All this time, I had but little food, principally fruit, which I found on the road. On Thursday night, I got into Salisbury, having left Chester on the Monday morning preceding. After this, being afraid my master was in pursuit of me, I left the usual line of road, and took another direction, through Huntsville and Salem, princi-pally through fields and woods; on my way to Caswell Court-House, a distance of nearly 200 miles from Salisbury,* I was stopped by a white man, to whom I told my old story, and again succeeded in my escape. I also came up with a small cart, driven by a poor man, who had been moving into some of the western territories, and was going back to Virginia, to move some more of his luggage. On this, I told him, I was going the same way to Hilton, thirteen miles from Caswell Court-House, he took me up in his cart, and we went to the Red House, two miles from Hilton, the place where Mr. Mitchell took me from, when six years old, to go to the Southern States. This was a very provi-dential circumstance, for it happened, that at the time I had to pass through Caswell Court-House, a fair or election was going on which caused the place to be much crowded with people, and rendered it more dangerous for me to pass through.

---

*The distance from Salisbury to Caswell Court-House is not so far, but I had to go a round about way.

At the Red House, I left the cart, and wandered about a long time, not knowing which way to go to find my mother. After some time, I took the road leading over Ikeo Creek. I shortly came up with a little girl, about six years old, and asked her where she was going, she said, to her mother's, pointing to a house on a hill, about half a mile off. She had been to the overseer's house, and was returning to her mother. I then felt some emotions arising in my breast, which I cannot describe, but will be fully explained in the sequel. I told her, that I was very thirsty, and would go with her to get something to drink. On our way, I asked her several questions, such, as her name, that of her mother, she said her's was Maria, and her mother's Nancy. I inquired, if her mother had any more children? she said, five besides herself, and that they had been told, that one had been sold when a little boy. I then asked, the name of this child? she said, it was Moses. These answers, as we approached the house, led me nearer and nearer to the finding out the object of my pursuit, and of recognizing in the little girl, the person of my own sister.* At last, I got to my mother's house!! my mother was at home, I asked her, if she knew me? she said, no. Her master was having a house built just by, and the men were digging a well, she supposed, that I was one of the diggers. I told her, I knew her very well, and thought that if she looked at me a little, she would know me, but this had no effect. I then asked her, if she had any sons? she said, yes; but none so large as me. I then waited a few minutes, and narrated some circumstances to her, attending my being sold into slavery, and how she grieved at my loss. Here the mother's feelings on that dire occasion, and which, a mother only can know, rushed to her mind: she saw her own son before her, for whom she had so often wept; and, in an instant, we were clasped in each other's arms, amidst the ardent

---

*Providence has been profuse in its blessings on me. When I wrote the foregoing statement, about my meeting with my sister Maria, and when I met with some who regarded this fact as bordering on the "marvellous," I little thought of such a proof of the truth of it, as I have now the pleasure of recording:—A gentleman of great respectability, at Manchester, having read the account in the first edition, has sent to America to purchase the freedom of Maria, and I know not, but she may be at this moment free, and is likely to be in this country in a short time.

interchange of caresses and tears of joy. Ten years had elapsed, since I had seen my dear mother. My own feelings, and the circumstances attending my coming home, have often been brought to mind since, on a perusal of the 42nd, 43rd, 44th, and 45th chapters of Genesis. What could picture my feelings so well, as I once more beheld the mother who had brought me into the world, and had nourished me, not with the anticipation of my being torn from her maternal care, when only six years old, to become the prey of a mercenary and blood-stained slaveholder; I say, what picture so vivid in description of this part of my tale, as the 7th and 8th verses of the 42nd chapter of Genesis, "And Joseph saw his brethren, and he knew them, but made himself strange unto them. And Joseph knew his brethren, but they knew not him." After the first emotion of the mother, on recognizing her first-born had somewhat subsided, could the reader not fancy the little one, my sister, as she told her simple tale of meeting with me to her mother, how she would say, while the parent listened with intense interest; "The man asked me straitly of our state and of our kindred, saying, is your father yet alive, and have ye another brother." Or, when at last, I could no longer refrain from making myself known, I say, I was ready to burst into a frenzy of joy. How applicable the 1st, 2nd, and 3rd verses of the 45th chapter, "Then Joseph could not refrain himself before all them that stood by him, and he wept aloud, and said unto his brethren, I am Joseph, doth my father still live." Then when the mother knew her son, when the brothers and sisters owned their brother; "he kissed all his brethren and wept over them, and after that his brethren talked with him," 15th verse. At night, my mother's husband, a blacksmith, belonging to Mr. Jefferson at the Red House, came home, he was surprised to see me with the family, not knowing who I was. He had been married to my mother, when I was a babe, and had always been very fond of me. After the same tale had been told him, and the same emotions filled his soul, he again kissed the object of his early affection. The next morning, I wanted to go on my journey, in order to make sure of my escape to the Free States. But, as might be expected, my mother, father, brothers, and sisters could ill part with their long lost one; and persuaded me to go into the woods in the day time, and at night come home and sleep there. This I did for about a week: on the next Sunday night, I had laid me down to sleep between my two brothers, on a pallet, which my mother had prepared for me; about twelve o'clock, I was suddenly awoke, and found my bed surrounded by twelve slave-holders with pistols in hand, who took me away (not allowing me to bid farewell to those I loved so dearly) to the Red House, where they confined me in a room the rest of the night, and in the morning, lodged me in the gaol of Caswell Court-House.

What was the scene at home, what sorrow possessed their hearts, I am unable to describe, as I never after saw any of them more. I heard, however, that my mother, who was in the family-way, when I went home, was soon after confined, and was very long before she recovered the effects of this disaster. I was told afterwards, that some of those men who took me, were profess-ing Christians, but to me, they did not seem to live up to what they professed; they did not seem, by their practices, at least, to recognize that God as their God, who hath said, "thou shalt not deliver unto his master, the servant which is escaped from his master unto thee, he shall dwell with thee, even among you, in that place which he shall choose, in one of thy gates, where it liketh him best; thou shalt not oppress him."—Deut. xxiii. 15, 16.

I was confined here in a dungeon under ground, the grating of which, looked to the door of the gaoler's house. His wife had a great antipathy to me. She was Mr. Roper's wife's cousin. My grandmother used to come to me nearly every day, and bring me something to eat, besides the regular gaol allowance, by which, my sufferings were somewhat decreased. Whenever the gaoler went out, which he often did, his wife used to come to my dun-geon, and shut the wooden door over the grating, by which, I was nearly suffocated, the place being very damp and noisome. My master did not hear of my being in gaol for thirty-one days after I had been placed there. He immediately sent his son, and son-in-law, Mr. Anderson, after me. They came in a horse and chaise, took me from the goal to a blacksmith's shop, and got an iron collar fitted round my neck, with a heavy chain attached,

then tied my hands, and fastened the other end of the chain on
another horse, and put me on its back. Just before we started,
my grandmother came to bid me farewell; I gave her my hand
as well as I could, and she having given me two or three presents, we parted. I had felt enough, far too much, for the weak
state I was in; but how shall I describe my feelings, upon part-
ing with the *last* relative that I *ever saw*. The reader must judge
by what would be his own feelings, under similar circumstances.
We then went on for fifty miles; I was very weak, and could
hardly sit on the horse. Having been in prison so long, I had lost
the southern tan; and, as the people could not see my hair, having my hat on, they thought I was a white man—a criminal—
and asked what crime I had committed. We arrived, late at
night, at the house of Mr. Britton. I shall never forget the journey that night. The thunder was one continued roar, and the
lightning blazing all around. I expected every minute, that my
iron collar would attract it, and I should be knocked off the
horse, and dragged along the ground. This gentleman, a year or
two before, had liberated his slaves, and sent them into Ohio,
having joined the Society of Friends, which Society does not
allow the holding of slaves. I was, therefore, treated very well
there, and they gave me a hearty supper, which did me much
good in my weak state.

They secured me, in the night, by locking me to the post of
the bed on which they slept. The next morning, we went on to
Salisbury. At that place, we stopped to water the horses; they
chained me to a tree in the yard, by the side of their chaise. On
my horse, they had put the saddle bags, which contained the
provisions. As I was in the yard, a black man came and asked
me, what I had been doing; I told him, I had run away from my
master, after which, he told me several tales about the slaves,
and among them, he mentioned the case of a Quaker, who was
then in prison, waiting to be hung, for giving a free pass to a
slave. I had been considering all the way, how I could escape
from my horse, and once had an idea of cutting his head off, but
thought it too cruel; and, at last, thought of trying to get a rasp,
and cut the chain by which I was fastened to the horse. As they
often let me get on nearly a quarter of a mile before them, I

thought, I should have a good opportunity of doing this without being seen. The black man procured me a rasp, and I put it into the saddle bags which contained the provisions. We then went on our journey, and one of the sons asked me, if I wanted any thing to eat; I answered, no, though very hungry at the time, as I was afraid of their going to the bags, and discovering the rasp. However, they had not had their own meal at the Inn, as I supposed, and went to the bags to supply themselves, where they discovered the rasp. Upon this, they fastened my horse beside the horse in their chaise, and kept a stricter watch over me. Nothing remarkable occurred, till we got within eight miles of Mr. Gooch's, where we stopped a short time; and, taking advantage of their absence, I broke a switch from some boughs above my head, lashed my horse, and set off at full speed. I had got about a quarter of a mile, before they could get their horse loose from their chaise; one, then rode the horse, and the other, ran as fast as he could after me. When I caught sight of them, I turned off the main road into the woods, hoping to escape their sight; their horse, however, being much swifter than mine, they soon got within a short distance of me. I then came to a rail fence, which I found it very difficult to get over, but breaking several rails away, I effected my object. They then called upon me to stop, more than three times, and I not doing so, they fired after me, but the pistol only snapped.

MR. ANDERSON ATTEMPTING TO SHOOT THE AUTHOR,
AFTER TELLING HIM TO STOP THREE TIMES, ACCORDING TO THE LAW.

This is according to law; after three calls, they may shoot a run-a-way slave. Soon after, the one on the horse came up with me, and, catching hold of the bridle of my horse, pushed the pistol to my side, the other soon came up; and, breaking off several stout branches from the trees, they gave me about 100 blows. They did this very near to a planter's house, the gentleman was not at home, but his wife came out, and begged them, not to *kill* me *so near the house;* they took no notice of this, but kept on beating me. They then fastened me to the axle-tree of their chaise, one of them got into the chaise, the other took my horse, and they run me all the eight miles as fast as they could; the one on my horse going behind to guard me. In this way, we came to my old master, Mr. Gooch. The first person I saw, was himself, he unchained me from the chaise, and, at first, seemed to treat me very gently, asking me, where I had been, &c. The first thing the sons did, was to show the rasp, which I had got to cut my chain. My master gave me a hearty dinner, the best he ever did give me, but it was to keep me from dying before he had given me all the flogging he intended. After dinner, he took me to a log-house, stripped me quite naked, fastened a rail up very high, tied my hands to the rail, fastened my feet together, put a rail between my feet, and stood on one end of it to hold it down; the two sons then gave me fifty lashes each, the son-in-law another fifty, and Mr. Gooch himself, fifty more.

While doing this, his wife came out, and begged him not to kill me, the first act of sympathy I ever noticed in her. When I called for water, they brought a pail-full and through it over my back, ploughed up by the lashes. After this, they took me to the blacksmith's shop, got *two large bars of iron,* which they bent round my feet, each bar *weighing twenty pounds,* and put a heavy log-chain on my neck. This was on Saturday. On the Monday, he chained me to the same female slave as before. As he had to go out that day, he did not give me the punishment which he intended to give me every day, but at night when he came home, he made us walk round his estate, and by all the houses of the slaves, for them to taunt us; when we came home, he told us, we must be up very early in the morning, and go to the fields before the other slaves. We were up at day-break, but we could not get on fast, on account of the heavy irons on my

MR. GOOCH STRIPPING THE AUTHOR TO FLOG HIM.
HIS TWO SONS AND SON-IN-LAW PRESENT.
THEY, AT THIS TIME, GAVE HIM FIFTY LASHES EACH.

feet. It may be necessary to state here, that these irons were first made red hot and bent in a circle, so as just to allow of my feet going through; it having been cooled, and my leg with the iron on lifted up to an anvil, it was made secure round my ancles. When I walked with these irons on, I used to hold them up with my hands by means of a cord. We walked *about a mile in two hours,* but knowing the punishment he was going to inflict on us, we made up our minds to escape into the woods, and secrete ourselves. This we did, and he not being able to find us, sent all his slaves, about forty, and his sons, to find us, which they could not do; and about twelve o'clock, when we thought, they would give up looking for us at that time, we went on, and came to the banks of the Catarba. Here I got a stone, and opening the ring of the chain on her neck, and got it off; and, as the chain round my neck was only passed through a ring, as soon as I had got her's off, I slipped the chain through my ring, and got it off my own neck.*—We then went on by the banks of the river for

*It may be well to state here, that the ring which fastened the log-chain together around the female's neck, was an open ring, similar to those used at the end of watch chains.

some distance, and found a little canoe about two feet wide. I
managed to get in, although the irons on my feet made it very
dangerous, for if I had upset the canoe, I could not swim. The
female got in after me, and gave me the paddles, by which we
got some distance down the river. The current being very
strong, it drove us against a small island; we paddled round the
island to the other side, and then made towards the opposite
bank. Here again we were stopped by the current, and made up
to a large rock in the river, between the island and the opposite
shore. As the weather was very rough, we landed on the rock
and secured the canoe, as it was not possible to get back to the
island. It was a very dark night and rained tremendously; and as
the water was rising rapidly towards the top of the rock, we gave
all up for lost, and sometimes hoped, and sometimes feared to
hope, that we should never see the morning. But Providence
was moving in our favour; the rain ceased, the water reached the
edge of the rock, then receded, and we were out of danger from
this cause. We remained all night upon the rock, and in the
morning reached the opposite shore, and then made our way
through the woods, till we came to a field of Indian corn, where
we plucked some of the green ears and eat them, having had
nothing for two days and nights. We came to the estate of ——,
where we met with a coloured man who knew me, and having
run away himself from a bad master, he gave us some food, and
told us, we might sleep in the barn that night. Being very
fatigued, we overslept ourselves; the proprietor came to the
barn, but as I was in one corner under some Indian corn tops,
and she is another, he did not perceive us, and we did not leave
the barn before night, (Wednesday). We then went out, got
something to eat, and strayed about the estate till Sunday. On
that day, I met with some men, one of whom, had had irons on
his feet the same as me, he told me, that his master was going
out to see his friends, and that he would try and get my feet
loose; for this purpose I parted with this female, fearing, that if
she were caught with me, she would be forced to tell who took
my irons off. The man tried some time without effect, he then
gave me a file and I tried myself, but was disappointed, on
account of their thickness.

On the Monday, I went on towards Lancaster, and got within three miles of it that night; and went towards the plantation of Mr. Crockett, as I knew some of his slaves, and hoped to get some food given me. When I got there, however, the dogs smelt me out and barked; upon which Mr. Crockett came out, followed me with his rifle, and came up with me. He put me on a horse's back, which put me to extreme pain, from the great weight hanging from my feet. We reached Lancaster gaol that night, and he lodged me there. I was placed in the next dungeon to a man who was going to be hung. I shall never forget his cries and groans, as he prayed all night for the mercy of God. Mr. Gooch did not hear of me for several weeks: when he did, he sent his son-in-law, Mr. Anderson after me. Mr. Gooch himself came within a mile of Lancaster, and waited until Mr. Anderson brought me. At this time, I had but one of the irons on my feet, having got so thin round my ankles, that I had slipped one off while in gaol. His son-in-law tied my hands, and made me walk along till we came to Mr. Gooch. As soon as we arrived at M'Daniel's Ford, two miles above the Ferry, on the Catarba River, they made me wade across, themselves going on horseback. The water was very deep, and having irons on one foot and round my neck, I could not keep a footing. They dragged me along by my chain, on the top of the water. It was as much as they could do to hold me by the chain, the current being very strong. They then took me home, flogged me, put extra irons on my neck and feet, and put me under the driver, with more work than ever I had before. He did not flog me so severely as before, but continued it every day. Among the instruments of torture employed, I here describe one:—

This is a machine used for packing and pressing cotton. By it, he hung me up by the hands at letter a, a horse moving round the screw e,* and carrying it up and down, and pressing the block c into the box d, into which the cotton is put. At this time, he hung me up for a quarter of an hour. I was carried up ten feet

*This screw is sometimes moved round by hand, when there is a handle on it. The screw is made with wood, a large tree cut down, and carved in the shape of a screw.

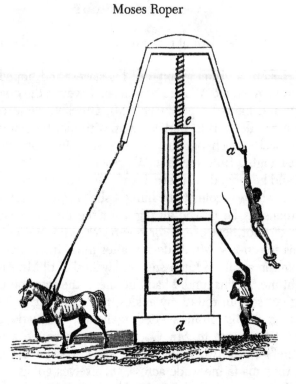

A COTTON SCREW.

from the ground, when Mr. Gooch asked me if I was tired. He then let me rest for five minutes, then carried me round again, after which, he let me down and put me into the box *d,* and shut me down in it for about ten minutes. After this torture, I stayed with him several months, and did my work very well. It was about the beginning of 1832, when he took off my irons, and being in dread of him, he having threatened me with more punishment, I attempted again to escape from him. At this time, I got into North Carolina: but a reward having been offered for me, a Mr. Robinson caught me, and chained me to a chair, upon which he sat up with me all night, and next day proceeded home with me. This was Saturday. Mr. Gooch had gone to church, several miles from his house. When he came back, the first thing he did was to pour some tar on my head, then rubbed it all over my face, took a torch, with pitch on, and set it on fire; he put it out before it did me very great injury, but the pain which I endured was most excruciating, nearly all my hair having been burnt off. On Monday, he put irons on me again, weighing nearly fifty pounds. He threatened me again on the Sunday with another flogging; and on the Monday morning, before day-break, I got away again, with my irons on, and was about three hours, going a distance of two miles.* I had gone a good distance, when I met with a coloured man, who got some wedges and took my irons off. However, I was caught again, and put into prison in Charlotte, where Mr. Gooch came, and took me back to Chester. He asked me, how I got my irons off? They having been got off by a slave, I would not answer his question, for fear of getting the man punished. Upon this, he put the fingers of my hands into a vice, and squeezed all my nails off. He then had my feet put on an anvil, and ordered a man to beat my toes, till he smashed some of my nails off. The marks of this treatment still remain upon me, some of my nails never having grown perfect since. He inflicted this punishment, in order to get out of me how I got my iron off, but never succeeded. After this, he hardly knew what to do with me; the whole stock of his cruelties seemed to be exhausted. He chained me down in the log-house. Soon after this, he sent a female slave to see if I was safe. Mr. Gooch had not secured me as he thought; but had only run my chain through the ring, without locking it. This I observed; and while the slave was coming, I was employed in loosening the chain with the hand that was not wounded. As soon as I observed her coming, I drew the chain up tight, and she observing, that I seemed fast, went away and told her master, who was in the field ordering the slaves. When she was gone, I drew the chain through the ring, escaped under the flooring of the log-house, and went on under it, till I came out at the other side, and ran on; but, being sore and weak, I had not got a mile before I was caught, and again carried back. He tied me up to a tree in the woods at night, and made his slaves flog me. I cannot say

---

*It must be recollected, that when a person is two miles from a house, in that part of the country, that he can hide himself in the woods, the trees being so thick.

how many lashes I received; but it was the worst flogging I ever had, and the last which Mr. Gooch ever gave me.

There are several circumstances which occurred on this estate while I was there, relative to other slaves, which it may be interesting to mention. Hardly a day ever passed without some one being flogged. To one of his female slaves he had given a dose of castor oil and salts together, as much as she could take; he then got a box, about six feet by two and a half, and one and a half feet deep; he put this slave under the box, and made the men fetch as many logs as they could get, and put them on the top of it: under this she was made to stay all night. I believe, that if he had given this slave one, he had given her three thousand lashes. Mr. Gooch was a member of a Baptist Church. His slaves thinking him a very bad sample of what a professing Christian ought to be, would not join the connexion he belonged to, thinking, they must be a very bad set of people: there were many of them members of the Methodist Church. On Sunday, the slaves can only go to church at the will of their master, when he gives them a pass for the time they are to be out. If they are found by the patrole after the time to which their pass extends, they are severely flogged.

On Sunday nights, a slave, named Allen, used to come to Mr. Gooch's estate for the purpose of exhorting and praying with his brother slaves, by whose instrumentality, many of them had been converted. One evening, Mr. Gooch caught them all in a room, turned Allen out, and threatened his slaves with one hundred lashes each, if they ever brought him there again. At one time, Mr. Gooch was ill, and confined to his room; if any of the slaves had done any thing, which he thought deserving a flogging, he would have them brought into his bed-room, and flogged before his eyes.

With respect to food, he used to allow us one peck of Indian meal each, per week, which, after being sifted, and the bran taken from it, would not be much more than half a peck. Meat we did not get for sometimes several weeks together; however, he was proverbial for giving his slaves more food than any other slave-holder. I stayed with Mr. Gooch a year and a half. During that time, the scenes of cruelty I witnessed and experienced, are not at all fitted for these pages. There is much to excite disgust in what has been narrated, but hundreds of other cases might be mentioned. After this, Mr. Gooch, seeing that I was determined to get away from him, chained me, and sent me with another female slave, whom he had treated very cruelly, to Mr. Britton, son of the before-mentioned, a slave dealer. We were to have gone to Georgia to be sold; but a bargain was struck before we arrived there. Mr. Britton had put chains on me to please Mr. Gooch; but having gone some little distance, we came up with a white man, who begged Mr. Britton to unchain me; he then took off my handcuffs. We then went on to Union Court-House, where we met a drove of slaves; the driver came to me, and ultimately bought me, and sent me to his drove; the girl was sold to a planter in the neighbourhood, as bad as Mr. Gooch. In court week, the negro traders and slaves encamp a little way out of the town. The traders here will often sleep with the best looking female slaves among them, and they will often have many children in the year, which are said to be slave-holder's children, by which means, through his villany, he will make an immense profit of this intercourse, by selling the babe with its mother. They often keep an immense stock of slaves on hand. Many of them will be with the trader a year or more, before they are sold. Mr. Marcus Rowland, the drover who bought me, then returned with his slaves to his brother's house (Mr. John Rowland), where he kept his drove on his way to Virginia. He kept me as a kind of servant. I had to grease the faces of the blacks every morning with sweet oil, to make them shine before they are put up to sell. After he had been round several weeks and sold many slaves, he left me, and some more, at his brother's house, while he went on to Washington, about 600 miles, to buy some more slaves, the drove having got very small. We were treated very well while there, having plenty to eat, and little work to do, in order to make us fat. I was brought up more as a domestic slave, as they generally prefer slaves of my colour for that purpose. When Mr. Rowland came back, having been absent about five months, he found all the slaves well, except one female, who had been grieving very much at being parted from her parents, and at last, died of grief. He dressed us very nicely, and went on again. I

travelled with him for a year, and had to look over the slaves, and
see that they were dressed well, had plenty of food, and to oil
their faces. During this time, we stopped once at White House
Church, a Baptist Association; a protracted camp meeting was
holding there, on the plan of the revival meetings in this country. We got there at the time of the meeting, and sold two female
slaves on the Sunday morning, at the time the meeting broke
up, to a gentleman who had been attending the meeting the
whole of the week. While I was with Mr. Rowland, we were at
many such meetings; and the members of the churches are by
this means so well influenced towards their fellow-creatures at
these meetings for the worship of God, that it becomes a fruit-
ful season for the drover, who carries on an immense traffic with
the attendants at these places. This is common to Baptists and
Methodists. At the end of the year, he exchanged me to a
farmer, Mr. David Goodley, for a female slave, in Greenville,
about fourteen miles from Greenville Court-House. The gentleman was going to Missouri to settle, and on his way, had to
pass through Ohio, a free state. But, having learnt, after he
bought me, that I had before tried to get away to the free states,
he was afraid to take me with him, and I was again exchanged to
a Mr. Marvel Louis. He was in the habit of travelling a great
deal, and took me as a domestic slave to wait on him. Mr. Louis
boarded me at the house of Mr. Clevelin, a very rich planter at
Greenville, South Carolina. Mr. L. was paying his addresses to
the daughter of this gentleman, but was surprised and routed in
his approaches by a Colonel Dorkins, of Union Court-House,
who ultimately carried her off in triumph. After this, Mr. Louis
took to drinking, to drown his recollection of disappointed love.
One day, he went to Pendleton Races, and I waited on the road
for him; returning intoxicated, he was thrown from his horse
into a brook, and was picked up by a gentleman, and taken to an
inn, and I went there to take care of him. Next day, he went on
to Punkintown with Mr. Warren R. Davis, a member of
Congress; I went with him. This was at the time of the agitation
of the Union and Nullifying party, which was expected to end in
a general war. The Nullifying party had a grand dinner on the
occasion, after which, they gave their slaves all the refuse, for

the purpose of bribing them to fight on the side of their party. The scene on this occasion was humourous, all the slaves scrambling after bare bones and crumbs, as if they had had nothing for months. When Mr. Louis had got over this fit of drunkenness, we returned to Greenville, where I had little to do, except in the warehouse. There was preaching in the Court-House on the Sunday; but scarcely had the sweet savour of the worship of God passed away, when, on Monday, a public auction was held for the sale of slaves, cattle, sugar, iron, &c. by Z. Davis, the high constable and others.

On these days, I was generally very busy in handing out the different articles for inspection, and was employed in this way for several months. After which, Mr. Louis left this place for Pendleton; but his health getting worse, and fast approaching consumption, he determined to travel. I went with him over Georgia to the Indian springs, and from there to Columbus; here he left me with Lawyer Kemp, a member of the State Assembly, to take care of his horses and carriage till he came back from Cuba, where he went for the benefit of his health. I travelled round with Mr. Kemp, waiting until my master came back. I soon after heard, that Mr. Louis had died at Appalachicola, and had been buried at Tennessee Bluff. I was very much attached to the neighbourhood of Pendleton and Greenville, and feared, from Mr. Louis's death, I should not get back there.

As soon as this information arrived, Mr. Kemp put me, the carriage and horses, a gold watch, and cigars, up to auction, on which I was much frightened, knowing there would be some very cruel masters at the sale; and fearing, I should again be disappointed in my attempt to escape from bondage. Mr. Beveridge, a Scotchman from Appalachicola, bought me, the horses, and cigars. He was not a cruel master; he had been in America eighteen years, and I believe, I was the first slave he ever bought. Mr. Kemp had no right to sell me, which he did, before he had written to Mr. Louis's brother.

Shortly after this, Mr. Kemp, having had some altercation with General Woodfork, it ended in a duel, in which Mr. W. was killed. A few weeks after, as Mr. Kemp, was passing down a street, he was suddenly shot dead by Mr. Milton, a rival lawyer.

When I heard this, I considered it a visitation of God on Mr. Kemp for having sold me unjustly, as I did not belong to him. This was soon discovered by me, Mr. Louis's brother having called at Mackintosh Hotel, Columbus, to claim me, but which he could not effect. After this, I travelled with Mr. Beveridge, through Georgia to the warm springs, and then came back to Columbus, going on to Marianna, his summer house, in Florida.

Here I met with better treatment than I had ever experienced before; we travelled on the whole summer; at the fall, Mr. Beveridge went to Appalachicola on business. Mr. Beveridge was contractor for the mail, from Columbus to Appalachicola, and owner of three steam boats, the Versailles, Andrew Jackson, and Van Buren. He made me steward on board the Versailles, the whole winter. The river then got so low, that the boats could not run. At this time Mr. Beveridge went to Mount Vernon. On our way, we had to pass through the Indian nation. We arrived at Columbus, where I was taken dangerously ill of a fever. After I got well, Mr. Beveridge returned to Marianna, through the Indian nation. Having gone about twelve miles, he was taken very ill. I took him out of the carriage to a brook, and washed his hands and face until he got better, when I got him into the carriage again, and drove off till we came to General Irving's, where he stopped several days, on account of his health. While there, I observed on the floor of the kitchen several children, one about three months old, without any body to take care of her; I asked, where her mother was, and was told, that Mrs. Irving had given her a very hard task to do at washing, in a brook, about a quarter of a mile distant. We heard after, that not being able to get it down, she had got some cords, tied them round her neck, climbed up a tree, swung off, and hung herself. Being missed, persons were sent after her, who observed several buzzards flying about a particular spot, to which they directed their steps, and found the poor woman nearly eaten up.

After this, we travelled several months without any thing remarkable taking place.

In the year 1834, Mr. Beveridge, who was now residing in

Appalachicola, a town in West Florida, became a bankrupt, when all his property was sold, and I fell into the hands of a very cruel master, Mr. Register, a planter in the same state; of whom, knowing his savage character, I always had a dread. Previously to his purchasing me, he had frequently taunted me, by saying, "You have been a gentleman long enough, and, whatever may be the consequences I intend to buy you." To which, I remarked, that I would, on no account, live with him, if I could help it. Nevertheless, intent upon his purpose, in the month of July, 1843, he bought me; after which, I was so exasperated, that I cared not whether I lived or died; in fact, whilst I was on my passage from Appalachicola, I procured a quart bottle of whiskey, for the purpose of so intoxicating myself, that I might be able, either to plunge myself into the river, or so to enrage my master, that he should dispatch me forthwith. I was, however, by a kind Providence, prevented from committing this horrid deed, by an old slave on board, who, knowing my intention, secretly took the bottle from me; after which, my hands were tied, and I was led into the town of Ochesa, to a warehouse, where my master was asked, by the proprietor of the place, the reason for his confining my hands, in answer to which, Mr. Register said, that he had purchased me. The proprietor, however, persuaded him to untie me; after which, my master being excessively drunk, asked for a cow hide, intending to flog me, from which, the proprietor dissuaded him, saying, that he had known me for some time, and he was sure, that I did not require to be flogged. From this place, we proceeded about mid-day on our way, he placing me on the bare back of a half-starved old horse, which he had purchased, and upon which sharp *surface*, he kindly intended, I should ride about eighty miles, the distance we were then from his home. In this unpleasant situation, I could not help reflecting upon the prospects before me, not forgetting, that I had heard, that my new master had been in the habit of stealing cattle, and other property, and among other things, a slave woman, and that I had said, as it afterwards turned out, in the hearing of some one who communicated the saying to my master, that I had been accustomed to live with a gentleman and not with a rogue; and, finding that he had been informed of this, I had the additional dread of a few hundred lashes for it, on my arrival at my destination.

About two hours after we started, it began to rain very heavily, and continued to do so, until we arrived at Marianna, about twelve at night, where we were to rest till morning. My master here questioned me, as to whether I intended to run away or not; and, I not then knowing the sin of lying, at once told him, that I would not. He then gave me his clothes to dry; I took them to the kitchen for that purpose, and he retired to bed, taking a bag of clothes belonging to me with him, as a kind of security, I presume, for my safety. In an hour or two afterwards, I took his clothes to him dried, and found him fast asleep. I placed them by his side, and said, that I would then take my own to dry too, taking care to speak loud enough, to ascertain whether he was asleep or not, knowing that he had a dirk and a pistol by his side, which he would not have hesitated using against me, if I had attempted secretly to have procured them. I was glad to find, that the effects of his drinking the day before had caused his sleeping very soundly, and I immediately resolved on making my escape; and without loss of time, started with my few clothes into the woods, which were in the immediate neighbourhood; and, after running many miles, I came to the river Chapoli, which is very deep, and so beset with aligators, that I dared not attempt to swim across. I paced up and down this river, with the hope of finding a conveyance across, for a whole day, the succeeding night, and till noon the following day, which was Saturday. About twelve o'clock on that day, I discovered an Indian canoe, which had not, from all appearance, been used for some time; this, of course, I used to convey myself across, and after being obliged to go a little way down the river, by means of a piece of wood, I providentially found in the boat, I landed on the opposite side. Here I found myself surrounded by planters looking for me, in consequence of which, I hid myself in the bushes until night, when I again travelled several miles, to the farm of a Mr. Robinson, a large sugar planter, where I rested till morning in a field. Afterwards I set out working my way through the woods, about twenty miles towards the east; this I knew by my knowledge of the position of the sun at its rising. Having reached the Chattahoochee river, which divides Florida from Georgia, I was again puzzled to know how to cross; it was three o'clock in the day, when a number of persons were fishing; having walked for some hours along the banks, I at last, after dark, procured a ferry-boat, which not being able, from the swiftness of the river, to steer direct across, I was carried many miles down the river, landing on the Georgian side, from whence I proceeded on through the woods two or three miles, and came to a little farm house about twelve at night; at a short distance from the house, I found an old slave hut, into which I went, and informed the old man, who appeared seventy or eighty years old, that I had had a very bad master, from whom I had run away; and asked him, if he could give me something to eat, having had no suitable food for three or four days; he told me, he had nothing but a piece of dry Indian bread, which he cheerfully gave me, having eaten it, I went on a short distance from the hut, and laid down in the wood to rest for an hour or two. All the following day (Monday), I continued travelling through the woods, was greatly distressed for want of water to quench my thirst, it being a very dry country, till I came to Spring Creek, which is a wide, deep stream, and with some of which, I gladly quenched my thirst. I then proceeded to cross the same, by a bridge close by, and continued my way until dusk. I came to a gentleman's house in the woods, where I inquired how far it was to the next house, taking care to watch an opportunity to ask some individual whom I could master, and get away from, if any interruption to my progress was attempted. I went on for some time, it being a very fine moonlight night, and was presently alarmed by the howling of a wolf very near me; which I concluded, was calling other wolves to join him in attacking me, having understood that they always assemble in numbers for such a purpose; the howling increased, and I was still pursued, and the numbers were evidently increasing fast; but I was happily rescued from my dreadful fright, by coming to some cattle, which attracted the wolves, and saved my life; for I could not get up the trees for safety, they being very tall pines, the lowest branches of which, were at least, forty or fifty feet from the ground, and the trunks very large and smooth.

About two o'clock, I came to the house of a Mr. Cherry, on
the borders of the Flint River; I went up to the house, and called
them up to beg something to eat; but having nothing cooked,
they kindly allowed me to lie down in the porch, where they
made me a bed. In conversation with this Mr. Cherry, I discovered that I had known him before, having been in a steam boat,
the Versaille, some months previous, which sunk very near his
house, but which I did not at first discern to be the same. I then
thought that it would not be prudent for me to stop there, and,
therefore, told them, I was in a hurry to get on, and must start
very early again, he having no idea who I was; and I gave his son
six cents to take me across the river, which he did when the sun
was about half an hour high, and unfortunately landed me
where there was a man building a boat, who knew me very well,
and my former master too,—he, calling me by name, asked me
where I was going.

I was very much frightened at being discovered, but sum-
moned up courage, and said, that my master had gone on to
Tallyhassa by the coach, and that there was not room for me,
and I had to walk round to meet him. I then asked the man to
put me in the best road to get there, which, however, I knew as
well as he did, having travelled there before; he directed me the
best way, but I of course took the contrary direction, wanting to
get on to Savannah. By this hasty and wicked deception, I saved
myself from going to Bainbridge prison, which was close by, and
to which, I should surely have been taken had it been known
that I was making my escape.

Leaving Bainbridge, I proceeded about forty miles, travelling
all day under a scorching sun, through the woods, in which I saw
many deer and serpents, until I reached Thomas Town in the
evening. I there inquired the way to Augusta, of a man whom I
met, and also asked where I could obtain lodgings, and was told
that there was a poor minister about a mile from the place who
would give me lodgings. I accordingly went, and found them in
a little log-house, where, having awakened the family, I found
them all lying on the bare boards, where I joined them, for the
remainder of the night.

In the morning, the old gentleman prayed for me that I might be preserved on my journey; he had previously asked me where I was going, and I knowing, that if I told him the right place, any that inquired of him for me would be able to find me, asked the way to Augusta, instead of Savannah, my real destination. I also told him, that I was partly Indian and partly white, but I am also partly African, but this I omitted to tell him, knowing if I did, I should be apprehended. After I had left this hut, I again inquired for Augusta, for the purpose of misleading my pursuers, but I afterwards took my course through the woods, and came into a road, called the Coffee road, which General Jackson cut down for his troops at the time of the war, between the Americans and Spaniards, in Florida; in which road there are but few houses, and which I preferred for the purpose of avoiding detection.

After several days I left this road, and took a more direct way to Savannah, where I had to wade through two rivers before I came to the Alatamah, which I crossed in a ferry-boat, about a mile below the place where the rivers Oconee and Ocmulgee run together into one river, called the Alatamah. I here met with some cattle drovers, who were collecting cattle to drive to Savannah. On walking on before them, I began to consider in what way I could obtain a passport for Savannah, and determined on the following plan:—

I called at a cottage, and after I had talked sometime with the wife, who began to feel greatly for me, in consequence of my telling her a little of my history, (her husband being out hunting) I pretended to shew her my passport, feeling for it everywhere about my coat and hat, and not finding it; I went back a little way pretending to look for it, but came back, saying, I was very sorry, but I did not know where it was. At last, the man came home, carrying a deer upon his shoulders, which he brought into the yard and began to dress it. The wife then went out to tell him my situation, and after long persuasion, he said he could not write, but that if I could tell his son what was in my passport, he should write me one; and knowing that I should not be able to pass Savannah without one, and having heard several free coloured men read theirs, I thought, I could tell the lad what to write. The lad sat down and wrote what I told him, nearly filling a large sheet of paper for the passport, and another sheet with recommendations. These being completed, I was invited to partake of some of the fresh venison, which the woman of the house had prepared for dinner, and having done so, and feeling grateful for their kindness, I proceeded on my way. Going along, I took my papers out of my pocket, and looking at them, although I could not read a word, I perceived that the boy's writing was very unlike other writing that I had seen, and was greatly blotted besides; consequently, I was afraid that these documents would not answer my purpose, and began to consider what other plan I could pursue to obtain another pass.

I had now to wade through another river to which I came, and which I had great difficulty in crossing, in consequence of the water overflowing the banks of several rivers to the extent of upwards of twenty miles. In the midst of the water, I passed one night upon a small island, and the next day, I went through the remainder of the water. On many occasions, I was obliged to walk upon my toes, and consequently, found the advantage of being six feet two inches high, (I have grown three inches since) and at other times was obliged to swim. In the middle of this extremity, I felt it would be imprudent for me to return; for if my master was in pursuit of me, my safest place from him was in the water, if I could keep my head above the surface. I was, however, dreadfully frightened, and most earnestly prayed that I might be kept from a watery grave, and resolved, that if again I landed, I would spend my life in the service of God.

Having, through mercy, again started on my journey, I met with the drovers; and having, whilst in the waters, taken the pass out of my hat, and so dipped it in the water as to spoil it, I showed it to the men, and asked them where I could get another. They told me, that in the neighbourhood, there lived a rich cotton-merchant who would write me one. They took me to him, and gave their word, that they saw the passport before it was wet, (for I had previously showed it to them,) upon which, the cotton-planter wrote a free pass and a recommendation, to which the cow-drovers affixed their marks.

The recommendation was as follows:

"John Roper, a very interesting young lad, whom I have seen

and travelled with for eighty or ninety miles on his road from Florida, is a free man, descended from Indian and white. I trust, he will be allowed to pass on without interruption, being convinced from what I have seen, that he is free, and though dark, is not an African. I had seen his papers before they were wetted."

These cow-drovers, who procured me the passport and recommendation from the cotton-planter, could not read; and they were intoxicated when they went with me to him. I am part African, as well as Indian and white, my father, being a white man, Henry Roper, Esq., Caswell County, North Carolina, U.S., a very wealthy slave-holder, who sold me when quite a child, for the strong resemblance I bore to him. My mother is part Indian, part African; but I dared not disclose that, or I should have been taken up. I then had eleven miles to go to Savannah, one of the greatest slave-holding cities in America, and where they are always looking out for run-a-way slaves. When at this city, I had travelled about five hundred miles.* It required great courage to pass through this place. I went through the main street with apparent confidence, though much alarmed; did not stop at any house in the city, but went down immediately to the Dock, and inquired for a berth, as a steward to a vessel to New York. I had been in this capacity before on the Appalachicola River. The person whom I asked to procure me a berth, was steward of one of the New York Packets; he knew Captain Deckay, of the schooner Fox, and got me a situation on board that vessel, in five minutes, after I had been at the Docks. The schooner Fox was a very old vessel, twenty-seven years old, laden with lumber and cattle for New York; she was rotten and could not be insured. The sailors were afraid of her; but I ventured on board, and five minutes after, we dropped from the Docks into the River. My spirits then began to revive, and I thought, I should get to a free country directly. We cast anchor in the stream, to keep the sailors on, as they were so dissatisfied with the vessel, and lay there four days; during which time, I had to go into the city

---

*The distance between these two places is much less than five hundred miles; but I was obliged to travel round about, in order to avoid being caught.

several times, which exposed me to great danger, as my master was after me, and I dreaded meeting with him in the city.

Fearing the Fox would not sail before I should be seized, I deserted her, and went on board a brig sailing to Providence, that was towed out by a steam boat, and got thirty miles from Savannah. During this time, I endeavoured to persuade the steward to take me as an assistant, and hoped to have accomplished my purpose; but the captain had observed me attentively, and thought I was a slave, he therefore ordered me, when the steam boat was sent back, to go on board her to Savannah, as the fine for taking a slave from that city to any of the free states, is five hundred dollars. I reluctantly went back to Savannah, among slave-holders and slaves. My mind was in a sad state; and I was under strong temptation to throw myself into the river. I had deserted the schooner Fox, and knew that the captain might put me into prison, till the vessel was ready to sail; if this had happened, and my master had come to the jail in search of me, I must have gone back to slavery. But when I reached the Docks at Savannah, the first person I met was the captain of the Fox, looking for another steward in my place. He was a very kind man, belonging to the free states, and inquired if I would go back to his vessel. This usage was very different to what I expected, and I gladly accepted his offer. This captain did not know that I was a slave. In about two days we sailed from Savannah to New York.

I am (August, 1834) unable to express the joy I now felt. I never was at sea before, and, after I had been out about an hour, was taken with sea-sickness, which continued five days. I was scarcely able to stand up, and one of the sailors was obliged to take my place. The captain was very kind to me all this time; but even after I recovered, I was not sufficiently well to do my duty properly, and could not give satisfaction to the sailors, who swore at me, and asked me why I shipped, as I was not used to the sea? We had a very quick passage; and in six days, after leaving Savannah, we were in the harbour at Statten Island, where the vessel was quarantined for two days, six miles from New York. The captain went to the city, but left me aboard with the sailors, who had most of them been brought up in the slave holding states, and were very cruel men. One of the sailors was particularly angry with me, because he had to perform the duties of my place; and while the captain was in the city, the sailors called me to the fore-hatch, where they said they would treat me. I went, and while I was talking, they threw a rope round my neck, and nearly choaked me. The blood streamed from my nose profusely. They also took up ropes with large knots, and knocked me over the head. They said, I was a negro; they despised me; and I expected they would have thrown me into the water. When we arrived at the city, these men, who had so ill treated me, ran away that they might escape the punishment, which would otherwise have been inflicted on them. When I arrived in the city of New York, I thought I was free; but learned I was not: and could be taken there. I went out into the country several miles, and tried to get employment; but failed, as I had no recommendation. I then returned to New York; but finding the same difficulty there to get work, as in the country, I went back to the vessel, which was to sail eighty miles up the Hudson River, to Poughkeepsie. When I arrived, I obtained employment at an inn, and after I had been there about two days, was seized with the cholera, which was at that place. The complaint was, without doubt, brought on by my having subsisted on fruit only, for several days, while I was in the slave states. The landlord of the inn came to me when I was in bed, suffering violently from cholera, and told me, he knew I had that complaint, and as it had never been in his house, I could not stop there any longer. No one would enter my room, except a young lady, who appeared very pious and amiable, and had visited persons with the cholera. She immediately procured me some medicine at her own expense, and administered it herself; and, whilst I was groaning with agony, the landlord came up and ordered me out of the house directly. Most of the persons in Poughkeepsie had retired for the night, and I lay under a shed on some cotton bales. The medicine relieved me, having been given so promptly; and next morning I went from the shed, and laid on the banks of the river below the city. Towards evening, I felt much better, and went on in a steam boat, to the city of Albany, about eighty miles. When I reached there, I went into

the country, and tried for three or four days to procure employment, but failed.

At that time, I had scarcely any money, and lived upon fruit,
so I returned to Albany, where I could get no work, as I could
not show the recommendations I possessed, which were only
from slave states, and I did not wish any one to know, I came
from them. After a time, I went up the western canal, as steward, in one of the boats. When I had gone about 350 miles up
the canal, I found I was going too much towards the slave states,
in consequence of which, I returned to Albany, and went up the
northern canal, into one of the New-England States—Vermont.
The distance I had travelled, including the 350 miles I had to
return from the west, and the 100 to Vermont, was 2,300 miles.
When I reached Vermont, I found the people very hospitable
and kind, they seemed opposed to slavery, so I told them, I was
a run-a-way slave. I hired myself to a firm in Sudbury.* After I
had been in Sudbury some time, the neighbouring farmers told
me, that I had hired myself for much less money than I ought. I
mentioned it to my employers, who were very angry about it; I
was advised to leave by some of the people round, who thought
the gentlemen I was with would write to my former master,
informing him where I was, and obtain the reward fixed upon
me. Fearing I should be taken, I immediately left, and went into
the town of Ludlow, where I met with a kind friend, Mr. ——,**
who sent me to school for several weeks. At this time, I was
advertised in the papers and was obliged to leave; I went a little
way out of Ludlow to a retired place, and lived two weeks with
a Mr. ——, deacon of a church at Ludlow; at this place, I could

---

*During my stay in this town, I thought of the vow I made in the water, (page
34,) and I became more thoughtful about the salvation of my soul. I attended
the Methodist Chapel, where a Mr. Benton preached, and there I began to
feel that I was a great sinner. During the latter part of my stay here, I became
more anxious about salvation, and I entertained the absurd notion that religion
would come to me in some extraordinary way. With this impression, I used to
go into the woods two hours before day-light to pray, and expected something
would take place, and I should become religious.

**It would not be proper to mention any names, as a person in any of the
States in America, found harbouring a slave, would have to pay a heavy fine.

have obtained education, had it been safe to have remained.*
From there, I went to New Hampshire, where I was not safe, so
went to Boston, Massachusetts, with the hope of returning to
Ludlow, to which place, I was much attached. At Boston, I met
with a friend, who kept a shop, and took me to assist him for several weeks. Here I did not consider myself safe, as persons from
all parts of the country were continually coming to the shop, and
I feared, some might come who knew me. I now had my head
shaved, and bought a wig, and engaged myself to a Mr. Perkins,
of Brookline, three miles from Boston, where I remained about
a month. Some of the family discovered that I wore a wig, and
said that I was a run-a-way slave; but the neighbours all round,
thought I was a white, to prove which, I have a document in my
possession to call me to military duty. The law is, that no slave
or coloured person performs this, but every other person, in
America, of the age of twenty-one, is called upon to perform
military duty, once or twice in the year, or pay a fine.

COPY OF THE DOCUMENT.

"Mr. Moses Roper,
"You being duly enrolled as a soldier in the Company, under
the command of Captain Benjamin Bradley, are hereby notified
and ordered to appear at the Town House, in Brookline, on
Friday, 28th instant, at 3 o'clock P.M., for the purpose of filling the
vacancy in said Company, occasioned by the promotion of Lieut.
Nathaniel M. Weeks, and of filling any other vacancy which may

---

*Whilst in this neighbourhood, I attended the Baptist Meeting, and trust the
preaching of the gospel was much blessed to my soul. As this was the first time
I was ever favoured with any education, I was very intent upon learning to read
the Bible, and in a few weeks, I was able, from my own reading, to repeat by
heart the whole of the last chapter of Matthew. I also attended the prayer and
inquiry meetings, where the attendants used to relate their experience, and I
was requested to do the same. I found these meetings a great blessing, and
they were the means, under God, of communicating to my mind a more clear
and distinct knowledge of the way of salvation by Jesus Christ.

then and there occur in said Company, and there wait further orders.

"By order of the Captain,

F. P. WENTWORTH, Clerk."

"Brookline, Aug. 14th, 1835."

I then returned to the city of Boston, to the shop where I was before.** Several weeks after I had returned to my situation, two coloured men informed me, that a gentleman had been inquiring for a person, whom, from the description, I knew to be myself, and offered them a considerable sum if they would disclose my place of abode; but they being much opposed to slavery, came and told me, upon which information, I secreted myself till I could get off. I went into the Green mountains for several weeks, from thence, to the city of New York, and remained in secret several days, till I heard of a ship, the Napoleon, sailing to England, and on the 11th of November, 1835, I sailed, taking with me letters of recommendation, to the Rev. Drs. Morison and Raffles, and the Rev. Alex. Fletcher. The time I first started from slavery, was in July, 1834, so that I was nearly sixteen months in making my escape.

On the 29th of November, 1835, I reached Liverpool, and my feelings when I first touched the shores of Britain were indescribable, and can only be properly understood by those who have escaped from the cruel bondage of slavery.

"'Tis liberty alone, that gives the flower of fleeting life

its lustre and perfume;

And we are weeds without it."

---

*Being very tall, I was taken to be twenty-one, but my correct age, as far as I can tell, is stated in page 3.

**During the first part of my abode in this city, I attended at the coloured church in Bellnap Street; and I hope, I found both profit and pleasure in attending the means of divine grace. I now saw the wicked part I had taken in using so much deception in making my escape. After a time, I found slave-owners were in the habit of going to this coloured chapel to look for run-a-way slaves. I became alarmed, and afterwards attended the preaching of the Rev. Dr. Sharp. I waited upon the Doctor to request he would baptize me, and admit me a member of his church; and after hearing my experience, he wished me to call again. This I did, but he was gone into the country, and I saw him no more.

"Slaves cannot breathe in England:
If their lungs receive our air, that moment they are free.
They touch our country and their shackles fall."—*Cowper.*

When I reached Liverpool, I proceeded to Dr. Raffles, and handed my letters of recommendation to him. He received me very kindly, and introduced me to a member of his church, with whom I stayed the night. Here I met with the greatest attention and kindness. The next day, I went on to Manchester, where I met with many kind friends, among others, Mr. Adshead, a Hosier of that town, to whom I desire, through this medium, to return my most sincere thanks for the many great services which he rendered me, adding both to my spiritual and temporal comfort. I would not, however, forget to remember here, Mr. Leese, Mr. Giles, Mr. Crewdson, and Mr. Clare, the latter of whom, gave me a letter to Mr. Scoble, the Secretary of the Anti-Slavery Society. I remained here several days, and then proceeded to London, December 12th, 1835, and immediately called on Mr. Scoble, to whom I delivered my letter, this gentleman procured me a lodging. I then lost no time in delivering my letters to Dr. Morison and the Rev. Alexander Fletcher, who received me with the greatest kindness, and shortly after this, Dr. Morison sent my letter from New York, with another from himself, to the *Patriot* Newspaper, in which, he kindly implored the sympathy of the public in my behalf. The appeal was read by Mr. Christopherson, a member of Dr. Morison's church, of which gentleman, I express but little of my feelings and gratitude, when I say, that throughout, he has been towards me a parent, and for whose tenderness and sympathy, I desire ever to feel that attachment which I do not know how to express.

I stayed at his house several weeks, being treated as one of the family. The appeal in the *Patriot,* referred to getting a suitable academy for me, which the Rev. Dr. Cox recommended at Hackney, where I remained half a year, going through the rudiments of an English education. At this time, I attended the ministry of Dr. Cox, which I enjoyed very much, and to which, I ascribe the attainment of clearer views of divine grace than I had before. I had attended here several months, when I expressed my wish to Dr. Cox, to become a member of his church, I was proposed, and after stating my experience was admitted, March 31st, 1836. Here I feel it a duty to present my tribute of thankfulness, however feebly expressed, to the affectionate and devoted attention of the Rev. Doctor, from whom, under God, I received very much indeed of spiritual advice and consolation, as well as a plentiful administration to my temporal necessities. I would not forget also to mention the kindness of his church generally, by whom I was received with Christian love and charity. Never, I trust, will be effaced from my memory, the parental care of the Rev. Dr. Morison, from whom I can strictly say, I received the greatest kindness I ever met with, and to whom, as long as God gives me lips to utter, or mind to reflect, I desire to attribute the comfort which I have experienced, since I set my foot upon the happy shores of England.

Here it is necessary that I should draw this narrative to a close, not that my materials are exhausted, but that I am unwilling to extend it to a size which might preclude many well-wishers from the possession of it.

But I must remark, that my feelings of happiness at having escaped from cruel bondage, are not unmixed with sorrow of a very touching kind. *"The land of the Free"* still contains the mother, the brothers, and the sisters of Moses Roper, not enjoying liberty, not the possessors of like feelings with me, not having even a distant glimpse of advancing towards freedom, but still slaves! This is a weight which hangs heavy on me. As circumstances at present stand, there is not much prospect of ever again seeing those dear ones—that dear mother, from whom, on the Sunday night, I was torn away by armed slave-holders, and carried into cruel bondage.* And, nothing would contribute so much to my entire happiness, if the kindness of a gracious Providence should ever place me in such favourable circumstances, as to be able to purchase the freedom of so beloved a parent. But I desire to express my entire resignation to the will of God. Should that Divine Being who made of one flesh all the kindreds of the earth, see fit that I should again clasp them to

---

*See page 15.

my breast, and see in them the reality of free men and free women, how shall I, a poor mortal, be enabled to sing a strain of praise sufficiently appropriate to such a boon from heaven.

But if the all-wise disposer of all things should see fit to keep them still in suffering and bondage, it is a mercy to know, that he orders all things well, that he is still the judge of all the earth, and that under such dispensations of his providence, he is working out that which shall be most for the advantage of his creatures.

Whatever I may have experienced in America, at the hands of cruel task-masters, yet I am unwilling to speak in any but respectful terms of the land of my birth. It is far from my wish to attempt to degrade America in the eyes of Britons. I love her institutions in the free States, her zeal for Christ; I bear no enmity even to the slave-holders, but regret their delusions, many I am aware are deeply sensible of the fault, but some I regret to say are not, and I could wish to open their eyes to their sin; may the period come, when God shall wipe off this deep stain from her constitution, and may America soon be *indeed* the land of the free.

In conclusion, I thank my dear friends in England for their affectionate attentions, and may God help me to show by my future walk in life, that I am not wanting in my acknowledgments of their kindness. But above all, to the God of all grace, I desire here before his people, to acknowledge that all the way in which he has led me, has been the right way, and as in his mercy and wisdom, he has led me to this country, where I am allowed to go free, may all my actions tend to lead me on, through the mercy of God in Christ, in the right way, to a city of habitation.

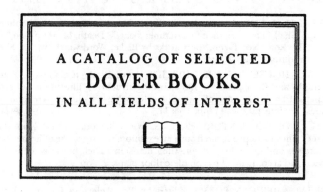

A CATALOG OF SELECTED
DOVER BOOKS
IN ALL FIELDS OF INTEREST

A CATALOG OF SELECTED DOVER
BOOKS IN ALL FIELDS OF INTEREST

100 BEST-LOVED POEMS, Edited by Philip Smith. "The Passionate Shepherd to His Love," "Shall I compare thee to a summer's day?" "Death, be not proud," "The Raven," "The Road Not Taken," plus works by Blake, Wordsworth, Byron, Shelley, Keats, many others. 96pp. 5³⁄₁₆ x 8¼.   0-486-28553-7

100 SMALL HOUSES OF THE THIRTIES, Brown-Blodgett Company. Exterior photographs and floor plans for 100 charming structures. Illustrations of models accompanied by descriptions of interiors, color schemes, closet space, and other amenities. 200 illustrations. 112pp. 8⅜ x 11.   0-486-44131-8

1000 TURN-OF-THE-CENTURY HOUSES: With Illustrations and Floor Plans, Herbert C. Chivers. Reproduced from a rare edition, this showcase of homes ranges from cottages and bungalows to sprawling mansions. Each house is meticulously illustrated and accompanied by complete floor plans. 256pp. 9⅜ x 12¼.

0-486-45596-3

101 GREAT AMERICAN POEMS, Edited by The American Poetry & Literacy Project. Rich treasury of verse from the 19th and 20th centuries includes works by Edgar Allan Poe, Robert Frost, Walt Whitman, Langston Hughes, Emily Dickinson, T. S. Eliot, other notables. 96pp. 5³⁄₁₆ x 8¼.   0-486-40158-8

101 GREAT SAMURAI PRINTS, Utagawa Kuniyoshi. Kuniyoshi was a master of the warrior woodblock print — and these 18th-century illustrations represent the pinnacle of his craft. Full-color portraits of renowned Japanese samurais pulse with movement, passion, and remarkably fine detail. 112pp. 8⅜ x 11.   0-486-46523-3

ABC OF BALLET, Janet Grosser. Clearly worded, abundantly illustrated little guide defines basic ballet-related terms: arabesque, battement, pas de chat, relevé, sissonne, many others. Pronunciation guide included. Excellent primer. 48pp. 4³⁄₁₆ x 5¾.

0-486-40871-X

ACCESSORIES OF DRESS: An Illustrated Encyclopedia, Katherine Lester and Bess Viola Oerke. Illustrations of hats, veils, wigs, cravats, shawls, shoes, gloves, and other accessories enhance an engaging commentary that reveals the humor and charm of the many-sided story of accessorized apparel. 644 figures and 59 plates. 608pp. 6⅛ x 9¼.

0-486-43378-1

ADVENTURES OF HUCKLEBERRY FINN, Mark Twain. Join Huck and Jim as their boyhood adventures along the Mississippi River lead them into a world of excitement, danger, and self-discovery. Humorous narrative, lyrical descriptions of the Mississippi valley, and memorable characters. 224pp. 5³⁄₁₆ x 8¼.   0-486-28061-6

ALICE STARMORE'S BOOK OF FAIR ISLE KNITTING, Alice Starmore. A noted designer from the region of Scotland's Fair Isle explores the history and techniques of this distinctive, stranded-color knitting style and provides copious illustrated instructions for 14 original knitwear designs. 208pp. 8⅜ x 10⅞.   0-486-47218-3

CATALOG OF DOVER BOOKS

ALICE'S ADVENTURES IN WONDERLAND, Lewis Carroll. Beloved classic about a little girl lost in a topsy-turvy land and her encounters with the White Rabbit, March Hare, Mad Hatter, Cheshire Cat, and other delightfully improbable characters. 42 illustrations by Sir John Tenniel. 96pp. 5¾₆ x 8¼.   0-486-27543-4

AMERICA'S LIGHTHOUSES: An Illustrated History, Francis Ross Holland. Profusely illustrated fact-filled survey of American lighthouses since 1716. Over 200 stations — East, Gulf, and West coasts, Great Lakes, Hawaii, Alaska, Puerto Rico, the Virgin Islands, and the Mississippi and St. Lawrence Rivers. 240pp. 8 x 10¾.
0-486-25576-X

AN ENCYCLOPEDIA OF THE VIOLIN, Alberto Bachmann. Translated by Frederick H. Martens. Introduction by Eugene Ysaye. First published in 1925, this renowned reference remains unsurpassed as a source of essential information, from construction and evolution to repertoire and technique. Includes a glossary and 73 illustrations. 496pp. 6⅛ x 9¼.   0-486-46618-3

ANIMALS: 1,419 Copyright-Free Illustrations of Mammals, Birds, Fish, Insects, etc., Selected by Jim Harter. Selected for its visual impact and ease of use, this outstanding collection of wood engravings presents over 1,000 species of animals in extremely lifelike poses. Includes mammals, birds, reptiles, amphibians, fish, insects, and other invertebrates. 284pp. 9 x 12.   0-486-23766-4

THE ANNALS, Tacitus. Translated by Alfred John Church and William Jackson Brodribb. This vital chronicle of Imperial Rome, written by the era's great historian, spans A.D. 14-68 and paints incisive psychological portraits of major figures, from Tiberius to Nero. 416pp. 5¾₆ x 8¼.   0-486-45236-0

ANTIGONE, Sophocles. Filled with passionate speeches and sensitive probing of moral and philosophical issues, this powerful and often-performed Greek drama reveals the grim fate that befalls the children of Oedipus. Footnotes. 64pp. 5¾₆ x 8 ¼.   0-486-27804-2

ART DECO DECORATIVE PATTERNS IN FULL COLOR, Christian Stoll. Reprinted from a rare 1910 portfolio, 160 sensuous and exotic images depict a breathtaking array of florals, geometrics, and abstracts — all elegant in their stark simplicity. 64pp. 8⅜ x 11.   0-486-44862-2

THE ARTHUR RACKHAM TREASURY: 86 Full-Color Illustrations, Arthur Rackham. Selected and Edited by Jeff A. Menges. A stunning treasury of 86 full-page plates span the famed English artist's career, from *Rip Van Winkle* (1905) to masterworks such as *Undine, A Midsummer Night's Dream,* and *Wind in the Willows* (1939). 96pp. 8⅜ x 11.
0-486-44685-9

THE AUTHENTIC GILBERT & SULLIVAN SONGBOOK, W. S. Gilbert and A. S. Sullivan. The most comprehensive collection available, this songbook includes selections from every one of Gilbert and Sullivan's light operas. Ninety-two numbers are presented uncut and unedited, and in their original keys. 410pp. 9 x 12.
0-486-23482-7

THE AWAKENING, Kate Chopin. First published in 1899, this controversial novel of a New Orleans wife's search for love outside a stifling marriage shocked readers. Today, it remains a first-rate narrative with superb characterization. New introductory Note. 128pp. 5¾₆ x 8¼.   0-486-27786-0

BASIC DRAWING, Louis Priscilla. Beginning with perspective, this commonsense manual progresses to the figure in movement, light and shade, anatomy, drapery, composition, trees and landscape, and outdoor sketching. Black-and-white illustrations throughout. 128pp. 8⅜ x 11.   0-486-45815-6

Browse over 9,000 books at www.doverpublications.com

THE BATTLES THAT CHANGED HISTORY, Fletcher Pratt. Historian profiles 16 crucial conflicts, ancient to modern, that changed the course of Western civilization. Gripping accounts of battles led by Alexander the Great, Joan of Arc, Ulysses S. Grant, other commanders. 27 maps. 352pp. 5⅜ x 8½.　0-486-41129-X

BEETHOVEN'S LETTERS, Ludwig van Beethoven. Edited by Dr. A. C. Kalischer. Features 457 letters to fellow musicians, friends, greats, patrons, and literary men. Reveals musical thoughts, quirks of personality, insights, and daily events. Includes 15 plates. 410pp. 5⅜ x 8½.　0-486-22769-3

BERNICE BOBS HER HAIR AND OTHER STORIES, F. Scott Fitzgerald. This brilliant anthology includes 6 of Fitzgerald's most popular stories: "The Diamond as Big as the Ritz," the title tale, "The Offshore Pirate," "The Ice Palace," "The Jelly Bean," and "May Day." 176pp. 5⅜ x 8½.　0-486-47049-0

BESLER'S BOOK OF FLOWERS AND PLANTS: 73 Full-Color Plates from Hortus Eystettensis, 1613, Basilius Besler. Here is a selection of magnificent plates from the *Hortus Eystettensis,* which vividly illustrated and identified the plants, flowers, and trees that thrived in the legendary German garden at Eichstätt. 80pp. 8⅜ x 11.
0-486-46005-3

THE BOOK OF KELLS, Edited by Blanche Cirker. Painstakingly reproduced from a rare facsimile edition, this volume contains full-page decorations, portraits, illustrations, plus a sampling of textual leaves with exquisite calligraphy and ornamentation. 32 full-color illustrations. 32pp. 9⅜ x 12¼.　0-486-24345-1

THE BOOK OF THE CROSSBOW: With an Additional Section on Catapults and Other Siege Engines, Ralph Payne-Gallwey. Fascinating study traces history and use of crossbow as military and sporting weapon, from Middle Ages to modern times. Also covers related weapons: balistas, catapults, Turkish bows, more. Over 240 illustrations. 400pp. 7¼ x 10⅛.　0-486-28720-3

THE BUNGALOW BOOK: Floor Plans and Photos of 112 Houses, 1910, Henry L. Wilson. Here are 112 of the most popular and economic blueprints of the early 20th century — plus an illustration or photograph of each completed house. A wonderful time capsule that still offers a wealth of valuable insights. 160pp. 8⅜ x 11.
0-486-45104-6

THE CALL OF THE WILD, Jack London. A classic novel of adventure, drawn from London's own experiences as a Klondike adventurer, relating the story of a heroic dog caught in the brutal life of the Alaska Gold Rush. Note. 64pp. 5³⁄₁₆ x 8¼.
0-486-26472-6

CANDIDE, Voltaire. Edited by Francois-Marie Arouet. One of the world's great satires since its first publication in 1759. Witty, caustic skewering of romance, science, philosophy, religion, government — nearly all human ideals and institutions. 112pp. 5³⁄₁₆ x 8¼.　0-486-26689-3

CELEBRATED IN THEIR TIME: Photographic Portraits from the George Grantham Bain Collection, Edited by Amy Pastan. With an Introduction by Michael Carlebach. Remarkable portrait gallery features 112 rare images of Albert Einstein, Charlie Chaplin, the Wright Brothers, Henry Ford, and other luminaries from the worlds of politics, art, entertainment, and industry. 128pp. 8⅜ x 11.　0-486-46754-6

CHARIOTS FOR APOLLO: The NASA History of Manned Lunar Spacecraft to 1969, Courtney G. Brooks, James M. Grimwood, and Loyd S. Swenson, Jr. This illustrated history by a trio of experts is the definitive reference on the Apollo spacecraft and lunar modules. It traces the vehicles' design, development, and operation in space. More than 100 photographs and illustrations. 576pp. 6¾ x 9¼. 0-486-46756-2

A CHRISTMAS CAROL, Charles Dickens. This engrossing tale relates Ebenezer Scrooge's ghostly journeys through Christmases past, present, and future and his ultimate transformation from a harsh and grasping old miser to a charitable and compassionate human being. 80pp. 5³⁄₁₆ x 8¼. 0-486-26865-9

COMMON SENSE, Thomas Paine. First published in January of 1776, this highly influential landmark document clearly and persuasively argued for American separation from Great Britain and paved the way for the Declaration of Independence. 64pp. 5³⁄₁₆ x 8¼. 0-486-29602-4

THE COMPLETE SHORT STORIES OF OSCAR WILDE, Oscar Wilde. Complete texts of "The Happy Prince and Other Tales," "A House of Pomegranates," "Lord Arthur Savile's Crime and Other Stories," "Poems in Prose," and "The Portrait of Mr. W. H." 208pp. 5³⁄₁₆ x 8¼. 0-486-45216-6

COMPLETE SONNETS, William Shakespeare. Over 150 exquisite poems deal with love, friendship, the tyranny of time, beauty's evanescence, death, and other themes in language of remarkable power, precision, and beauty. Glossary of archaic terms. 80pp. 5³⁄₁₆ x 8¼. 0-486-26686-9

THE COUNT OF MONTE CRISTO: Abridged Edition, Alexandre Dumas. Falsely accused of treason, Edmond Dantès is imprisoned in the bleak Chateau d'If. After a hair-raising escape, he launches an elaborate plot to extract a bitter revenge against those who betrayed him. 448pp. 5³⁄₁₆ x 8¼. 0-486-45643-9

CRAFTSMAN BUNGALOWS: Designs from the Pacific Northwest, Yoho & Merritt. This reprint of a rare catalog, showcasing the charming simplicity and cozy style of Craftsman bungalows, is filled with photos of completed homes, plus floor plans and estimated costs. An indispensable resource for architects, historians, and illustrators. 112pp. 10 x 7. 0-486-46875-5

CRAFTSMAN BUNGALOWS: 59 Homes from "The Craftsman," Edited by Gustav Stickley. Best and most attractive designs from Arts and Crafts Movement publication — 1903–1916 — includes sketches, photographs of homes, floor plans, descriptive text. 128pp. 8¼ x 11. 0-486-25829-7

CRIME AND PUNISHMENT, Fyodor Dostoyevsky. Translated by Constance Garnett. Supreme masterpiece tells the story of Raskolnikov, a student tormented by his own thoughts after he murders an old woman. Overwhelmed by guilt and terror, he confesses and goes to prison. 480pp. 5³⁄₁₆ x 8¼. 0-486-41587-2

THE DECLARATION OF INDEPENDENCE AND OTHER GREAT DOCUMENTS OF AMERICAN HISTORY: 1775-1865, Edited by John Grafton. Thirteen compelling and influential documents: Henry's "Give Me Liberty or Give Me Death," Declaration of Independence, The Constitution, Washington's First Inaugural Address, The Monroe Doctrine, The Emancipation Proclamation, Gettysburg Address, more. 64pp. 5³⁄₁₆ x 8¼. 0-486-41124-9

THE DESERT AND THE SOWN: Travels in Palestine and Syria, Gertrude Bell. "The female Lawrence of Arabia," Gertrude Bell wrote captivating, perceptive accounts of her travels in the Middle East. This intriguing narrative, accompanied by 160 photos, traces her 1905 sojourn in Lebanon, Syria, and Palestine. 368pp. 5⅜ x 8½. 0-486-46876-3

A DOLL'S HOUSE, Henrik Ibsen. Ibsen's best-known play displays his genius for realistic prose drama. An expression of women's rights, the play climaxes when the central character, Nora, rejects a smothering marriage and life in "a doll's house." 80pp. 5³⁄₁₆ x 8¼. 0-486-27062-9